A Woman with a Minute...

A Woman with a Minute...

Barbara Stoker

**Andrews McMeel
Publishing**

Kansas City

06 07 08 09 10 SDB 10 9 8 7 6 5 4 3 2 1

ISBN-13: 978-0-7407-5741-9
ISBN-10: 0-7407-5741-5

Library of Congress Control Number: 2005933220

www.andrewsmcmeel.com

www.awomanwithaminute.com

Illustrations by Anita Bartlett

*This book is dedicated to you, the reader,
and all of the fabulous women out there
who work magic with every minute.*

Please give yourself the credit you deserve.

*A*cknowledgments

Connor, I appreciate all of your creative direction. Nick, I'm grateful for your careful crafting of words. Joey, your sense of humor added a lot to this book. I would like to thank all three of you for your unwavering love, faith, and support. I am very lucky to have you in my life. Trigby, Scandi, and Pounder, you've taught all of us about unconditional love.

Valari, it is through your wisdom that I have learned so many valuable lessons about life, love, and laughter. Thank you for staying close to me even now. You continue to be my inspiration and twin spirit.

Anita, you are amazing. Thank you for taking my vision and translating it into such fun illustrations. You are a delight to work with and I'm grateful for the fabulous energy you brought to this project.

Suzy, where would I be without you? Julie, your counsel has kept me on the straight if not narrow path. Brian, thank you for being my champion. I thank all of you for the unqualified friendship you continue to provide.

I would like to thank Patty at Andrews McMeel, Doris at DSM Agency, and Margaret at the unparalleled Tattered Cover for seeing the potential in this book.

There are many people who have helped me climb the mountains in my life. A special thanks to Barb, Cami, Cathy, Dad, Diane, Doug, Grandma Miller, Judith, Laura, Leslie, Loneta, Mom, Neal, Ruthie, and Shayna.

*O*nce upon a time I wondered why I was the only one who always seemed so far behind in everything. I'd ask myself over and over again, "How does everyone else do it all?" I wondered what was wrong with me, because no matter how fast I went or how hard I worked I could never seem to get caught up. I was operating under the very mistaken assumption that everyone except me was just about perfect. I started to believe that I was the only woman out there living a fragmented life—misplacing, losing, and forgetting things at an astonishing rate. Yet on the rare occasion when I would actually stop and think about it, I would realize that despite it all, I was actually getting an amazing number of things done.

At this point I started asking other women about their days. I found that once we got past the superficial, "I'm fine, my job is wonderful, and my children are perfect," almost everyone's life was similar to mine. No matter the women's nationality, whether or not they had children, whether or not they worked outside of the home, whether or not they were married—all of us had way too much to do, not enough time to do it, and no matter how much we got done, we all felt as if we were getting further and further behind.

At times women may seem to go about things in a somewhat unorganized, unconventional, and unorthodox way, yet somehow we still get an absolutely amazing amount accomplished. We are proof that the Chaos Theory works.

The moral of this story is that no one is perfect. In fact, perfection is positively boring and leaves no room for excitement and spontaneity. Today's woman lives a demanding life, and each of us needs to realize we are doing an exceptional job. We are sharp, smart, and sophisticated individuals who are making it happen. So let's give ourselves credit and start living happily (not perfectly) ever after!

A Woman with a Minute...

will want to sit down
in her favorite chair.

However, first she
may want to . . .

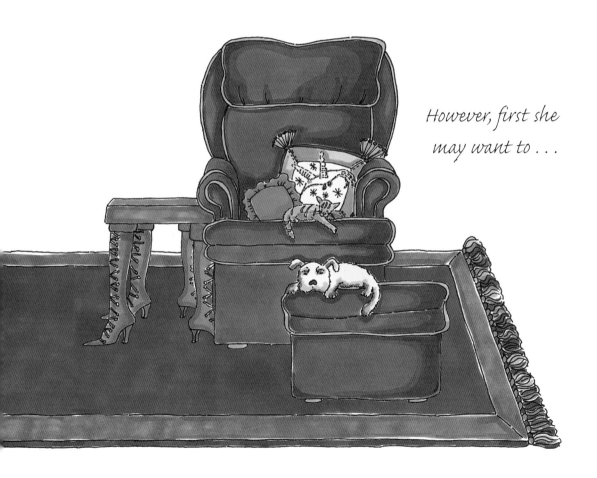

... get a cup of coffee. If there isn't any coffee ready she'll start to make some. That's when she'll see the notes.

They will remind her to deliver the soup to her sick friend and that she still needs to make something for the bake sale today. She'll secretly wish that she had simply ordered something from the bakery.

As the coffee brews, she'll look for a gourmet cookie recipe. Settling for the recipe on the back of the chocolate chip bag she'll realize that she needs her glasses to read it. She'll start searching for them.

As she sees her reflection in the microwave she'll realize that they were on top of her head the whole time.

As she reads the recipe she'll decide to start getting out the ingredients.

If she can't find all the ingredients, that will remind her that there are still some groceries in the car.

On her way to the garage she'll walk past the laundry room and decide to throw some clothes into the washer.

When the light in the garage goes out, she'll change the bulb, which is when she may see the drill.

The drill will remind her that the latch on the back door is loose.

As she's tightening the latch the phone will probably ring. If it does, she'll run into the house to answer it.

If the phone is missing she'll
follow the ringing sound to find it.

As she searches for the phone she'll think
about how she should call her mom. When she finds the
phone, the call will be a reminder for the fund-raising
dinner she's to attend that evening.

She may also find the TV remote and her missing charm bracelet, the one she got on her birthday. That will remind her of her friend's upcoming birthday and that she needs to get her present into the mail today. She'll go look for the gift she purchased weeks ago.

Once she finds the present,
she'll head to the
basement to wrap it.

As she starts wrapping the present she'll need scissors. If she can't find them, she'll go back upstairs to look for them.

Once she gets to the kitchen she may wonder, "Why did I come up here?" That's when she'll see the coffeepot, which will remind her that she wanted a cup of coffee. Since it's cold she'll put a cup in the microwave.

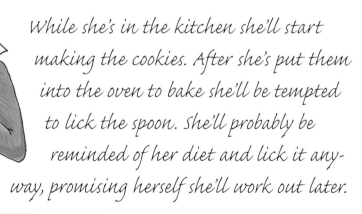

While she's in the kitchen she'll start making the cookies. After she's put them into the oven to bake she'll be tempted to lick the spoon. She'll probably be reminded of her diet and lick it any-way, promising herself she'll work out later.

With the cookies in the oven, she'll head back to her chair with a hot cup of coffee, kicking off her shoes. As cute as they are, they have never been very comfortable.

As she sets the coffee cup down on the table she may hear, "You've got mail." That will remind her that she hasn't checked any of her e-mails, so she'll go to her desk.

As she's reading her e-mails, she'll hear a beep coming from her cell phone, letting her know that the battery is low, so she'll put it into the charger. As she does, she may notice the stack of mail, which will remind her that she needs to pay bills.

To make sure she avoids any late charges, she'll probably start writing checks. Once she's done she'll look for stamps. This is when she'll find the scissors. They will remind her of the present she needs to finish wrapping, so she'll head back down to the basement.

After she's finished wrapping the present she'll put on a mailing label, which will remind her she needs postage, so . . .

she'll go all the way back upstairs to look for stamps.

As she walks through the kitchen she'll remember her coffee. When she can't find her cup she'll fill up a new one and put it in the microwave.

That's when the timer will go off for the cookies. She'll check and decide they need a few more minutes.

With the cookies back in the oven, she'll head to her chair with a new cup of coffee. That's when she'll pick up the report, which will remind her that she wanted to print out an extra copy. So she'll go back to her desk.

As she starts to print out the extra copy of
the report she'll see the bills, and
start looking for
the stamps again.

That's when she may smell something, which will remind her that she forgot all about the cookies, so she'll run into the kitchen.

The burnt cookies will make her want to kick herself for not ordering from the bakery. She'll begin to wonder if anyone will notice if she doesn't bring anything. Then her conscience will take over and she'll make a note to call the bakery. She may feel a little guilty about not making something herself, so she'll plan to take a tray for the cookies, in hopes that they'll look more like homemade.

She'll turn on the water in the sink and put the cookie sheet in to soak so that it'll be easier to wash later. That's when the doorbell will ring and she'll run to answer it.

If it's a neighbor circulating a petition they'll discuss the need for everyone to take more action. Feeling like she should get involved, she'll agree to help by getting more signatures. Then she'll go back to the kitchen.

She knew she should have ordered from the bakery! Just as she finishes mopping the floor she'll hear the alarm on her computer, reminding her that it's time to get ready for her board meeting.

So she'll run upstairs to change.

That's when she'll remember that she had dropped off her favorite suit at the cleaners, requesting overnight service, and forgot to pick it up.

She'll look for something else to wear.

Once she's ready to go,
she'll look for her car keys.

If they aren't in her bag, she'll look through the pockets of her coats in the hall closet.

As she's looking she may come across a stack of books that she has never finished reading. If she does, she'll push them a little farther back into the closet.

Once she finds her keys she'll grab the soup, the tray, the package, the bills, her workout bag, her laptop, and the reports. Then she'll head out to the car. When she walks past the laundry room, she'll think about the clothes in the washer.

She'll probably run back into the house to put the clothes into the dryer.

Before she backs out of the driveway, she'll remember that she needs to order cookies from the bakery. So she'll look for her cell phone and remember that she left it in the charger. She'll run back into the house again.

As she walks in she'll notice that the flowers in the vase need water, so she'll take them into the kitchen with her.

Once she's in the kitchen she'll remember that she never got that cup of coffee. She'll put a to-go cup in the microwave.

So that she doesn't waste sixty seconds she'll go to get her cell phone out of the charger. When she picks it up she'll notice the time, which will remind her she'd better leave for her meeting.

As she goes out the front door she may walk past her favorite chair and smile wistfully.

Since she doesn't have time to run
her errands, she'll head straight to
her meeting. Once the update
begins she'll blind everyone with
her brilliant, succinct analysis
of the current situation as
she covers every possible
contingency, financial scenario,
and anticipated reaction.

She'll leave the meeting focused on her success, until she reaches her car. That's when she'll notice her workout bag, which will remind her that she hasn't exercised all week.

Feeling guilty, she'll drive straight to the gym. As soon as she changes into her sweats a friend may ask her how the bake sale went. That will remind her that she hasn't picked up the cookies from the bakery and it closes in ten minutes. With no time left to work out, she'll run to the bakery.

When she walks into the bakery the smell of baking bread will remind her of home and that she needs to call her mom.

She'll call her mom from the car. She'll get so involved in the conversation that she'll drive right past the bake sale, so she'll turn around and go back.

Since she didn't have time for lunch, she'll be starving and tempted to eat all the cookies. However, remembering her diet, she'll keep only a few for herself. The rest she'll take out of the bakery box and put on the tray.

At the bake sale someone may ask how her sick friend is feeling, which will remind her that she needs to drop off the soup. When she delivers it, her friend may ask about the fund-raiser that evening, which will remind her to go to the cleaners.

As she's picking up her cleaning, the owner may mention that her suit has been ready for several days, suggesting that she only request "rush service" if she needs it. Since they are always so accommodating, she'll feel bad and give them all the cookies she had kept for herself.

As she pays for her dry cleaning she'll be reminded to mail the bills and the birthday present.

Since the mailbox is right next to a coffee shop, she'll decide to run in and treat herself to a tall, nonfat, sugar-free vanilla latte with an extra shot of espresso.

Seeing the line, she may decide not to go in. That's when she'll notice the new little boutique next door. That will remind her of the fundraiser and that she really doesn't have anything quite right to wear.

So, she may . . .

. . . go shopping.

When the shop starts closing she'll realize it's time to head straight home.

When she finally gets home she'll immediately start getting ready for the fund-raiser.

Once she's dressed,

all she'll want to do is sit down in her favorite chair.

However, first she may want to . . .

. . . get a glass of wine.

That's when the phone will probably ring . . .

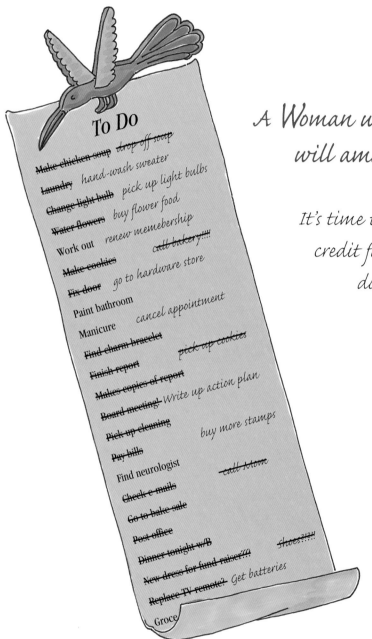

To Do

Make chicken soup   drop off soup
Laundry   hand-wash sweater
Change light bulb   pick up light bulbs
Water flowers   buy flower food
Work out   renew memebership
Make cookies   call bakery!!!!
Fix door   go to hardware store
Paint bathroom
Manicure   cancel appointment
Find charm bracelet
Finish report   pick up cookies
Makes copies of report
Board meeting!   Write up action plan
Pick up cleaning
Pay bills   buy more stamps
Find neurologist   call Mom
Check e-mails
Go to bake sale
Post office
Dinner tonight w/B   shoes?!?!
New dress for fund raiser???
Replace TV remote?   Get batteries
Groce

A Woman with a Minute...
will amaze you.

It's time to give yourself more
credit for all that you get
done in a day!

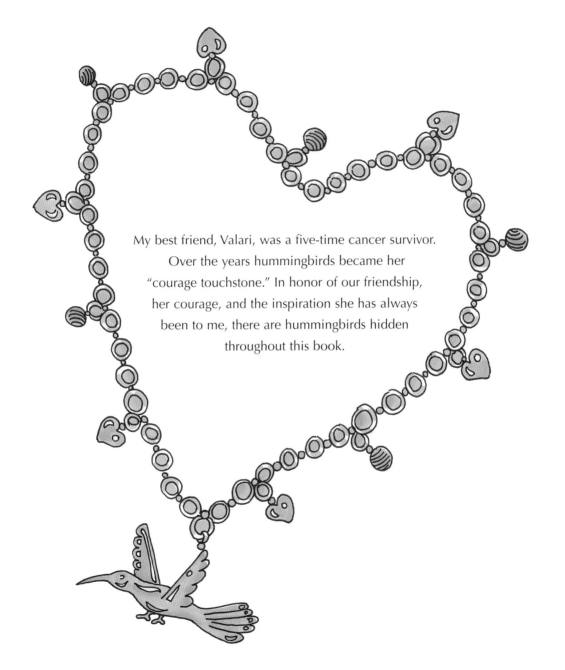

My best friend, Valari, was a five-time cancer survivor.
Over the years hummingbirds became her
"courage touchstone." In honor of our friendship,
her courage, and the inspiration she has always
been to me, there are hummingbirds hidden
throughout this book.

My Story

Why did I write this book? I wanted to help women everywhere (including myself) put their lives in perspective. I wanted women to understand and value all they do in a day. I believe that it's important that we stop holding ourselves up to an unrealistic and ridiculous standard of perfection. It's time to let go of the craziness we allow ourselves to get caught up in and lighten up, a lesson I learned in an interesting way.

About a year ago, I had a week that really scared me. At the end of seven days I had lost a two-carat diamond ring, a credit card, my driver's license, and my cell phone—twice. I had been worried about my forgetfulness, but now it was time to take action, so I decided to see a neurologist. I had to face up to whatever terrible disease was stealing my mind.

I, of course, researched and found one of the best neurologists in the Denver area. She asked me to take a number of sophisticated tests, which all came back normal. That's when she asked me to describe my life. I told her I was a single mom with three sons. We had a new kitten, Scandi, and a dog named Pounder, who had just undergone extensive reconstructive surgery on his leg.

She asked about my job. I told her that I worked full-time from home, that I traveled a fair bit, and that I was doing research and writing a book on women and intelligent risk taking. Then she asked what I did in my spare time. I asked her to define "spare time." She described it as any time left over when I wasn't sleeping. I told her I was involved in the boys' school, their activities, and their sports. She asked about my passions. I shared that I was a Wish Grantor for the Make-A-Wish

Foundation and that I loved to climb, plus I had just become a paragliding pilot.

When she inquired about how old my sons were, I simply opened the door for her to see for herself. Since I hadn't found anyone brave enough to watch them that day, I had been forced to bring them with me.

Joey (ten) had climbed up on the windowsill and was looking upside down into the aquarium, making bizarre faces and noises at the fish. Nick (twelve) was launching a full-scale military assault with at least a hundred G.I. Joes that he had set up on the chairs, tables, and floor. Connor (thirteen) had draped himself across the couch in torn-up black clothes and was reading a skater magazine and listening to heavy-metal music through his headphones. His music was so loud that we could hear it all the way back in the examination room.

Fortunately for me, the neurologist had a sense of humor. She looked at me and told me I had two options: lose the kids or simplify my life. I have tried both with mediocre success.

To this day my ring is still missing. I found my credit card at Krispy Kreme when I drove through for a quick snack on my way to a workout. My driver's license turned up at the gym (I had to use it to get in, since I couldn't find my membership card). I called my own cell phone just to see if anyone would answer it. Mark, from the express lane at the grocery store, said, "Hello." He remembered me clearly; I was the lady with sixteen items in the line for ten items or fewer. He said he had also found my membership card to the gym.

Two days after I had recovered my cell phone, I got a call in my office. The caller

ID said the number was the same as my cell phone. Wondering why my caller ID wasn't working, I picked up the call. It turned out that some honest soul was calling me from my own cell phone. She'd found it in the parking lot of my sons' school. This was quite a surprise, since I had not yet realized that I had lost it.

I have truly tried my neurologist's options. I've tried losing the boys several times, but they keep finding their way back home. And I've tried to simplify my life. That hasn't gone very well either, as every day things seem to get more complicated, with more demands.

I travel all over the world, lecturing and consulting on intelligent risk taking. For the past ten years I have focused on women and risk. I set out to discover why intelligent, capable women are so often reluctant to take the risks required for success. Although I arrived at no simple answers, I have discovered that a unique phenomenon takes place with women. We know intellectually that we are talented and that we want our talents, strengths, and success to be valued by others. Yet, too often, we are the ones who ignore our strengths, play down our successes, focus on our mistakes, devalue our own accomplishments, and refuse to give ourselves the credit we've earned, which in turn undermines our self-confidence. We constantly hold ourselves up to an unrealistic standard of perfection and find ourselves lacking. If we have a hundred things on our to-do list and get ninety-five done, most of us will still go to bed frustrated by what we didn't accomplish.

I see this phenomenon in myself and in other women, so I decided to write two books to help women make a shift: this book, which takes a fun, lighthearted approach, and a second book, *Positive Risk,* which takes a more serious look at how to take intelligent risks.

My challenge (to all of us) is that we start giving ourselves credit, acknowledge how very talented we are, and then go take those risks that will make a difference in our lives and in the lives of others. Tonight, try focusing on how much you got done today. Think about what you're proud of, it would be even better if you said it out loud, and it would be great if you told someone else how awesome you were today.

*A special acknowledgment to all the exceptional children
I have had the honor and privilege of getting to know through
the Make-A-Wish Foundation.*

Thank you for teaching me to measure life in memories.

Barbara, Your Princess Servant

Hummingbird

I dreamt I was a Hummingbird
A dream quite simply so absurd
So audacious on my part,
To compare myself to nature's art.

Undaunted, fearless, in spite of size
This flying jewel sweeps the skies
God's creation—our delight
Perhaps they're angels in constant flight.

by Valari Burger, December 2001